GARDENS ILLUSTRATED

KNOW HOW

PRUNING

THE RIGHT CUT

by

PENELOPE HOBHOUSE

JOHN BROWN PUBLISHING

FOREWORD

Most gardening techniques are very simple and can be discovered by using common sense and imagination. Getting the soil right is the first priority. Good, well-prepared tilth with plenty of earthworms is obviously going to give plants a good start. If the worms are happy plants will probably thrive. Planting correctly is another essential. This includes choosing plants with well-developed root systems, and avoiding those which have been badly grown or are pot-bound. Each plant or group of plants must have the right soil and climatic conditions. It is no use planting acid-loving plants in alkaline soil or planting the moisture lovers where they will dry out.

Established woody plants need pruning and training, often on an annual basis, and most soft-stemmed perennials need dividing in order to maintain their vigour. The most fun in gardening comes from making new plants from old; propagating from cuttings and growing newplants or replacements from seed.

Gardening carefully and thoughtfully brings its own rewards. The pleasure of watching things grow, waiting patiently, not hurrying results, that is the best way to gain experience. Like the garden itself, gardening know-how grows with time.

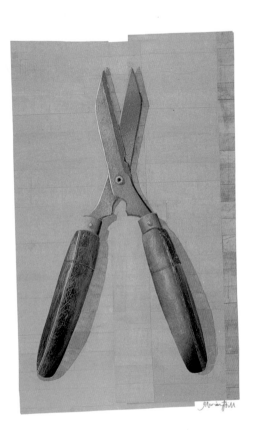

For any gardener, it is essential to grasp certain basic facts about why we have to prune at all. It might seem more obvious to allow nature just to take its course. In their wild setting, given time, dead or diseased branches will naturally fall from trees and shrubs. But plants in a garden, where soil has been specially prepared and is often richer than in their natural habitat, have to perform for us

TRADITIONALLY-SHAPED, sharp shears are essential tools for cutting and trimming hedges and for shaping topiary.

in a more purposeful way. We want them to flower regularly each year, have good, healthy, fresh foliage with no diseased or misshapen branches, and we want them to look orderly and graceful when they are not in flower. Also in the average garden we may be short of space and pruning can lift the heads of plants, to allow other plants to thrive around their base. Quite a few untidy-growing shrubs such as berberis are much improved if clipped into a regular shape for the second half of the summer season

Unless we grow them for their decorative fruits, it may be wise to save the plant the effort of setting seed, so judicious removal of dead flowering branches and dead flowers will help garden plants – both woody and herbaceous - to retain their vigour. Fruit trees bred for maximum production need to be trained into a framework of fruiting spurs. Trees and shrubs, if allowed to grow unchecked, can grow too large for their garden situations, and unfortunately pruning promotes even faster growth. Specimen trees, must be carefully selected so that their eventual size is right for the available site; regular pruning will only give them an ugly shape. On the other hand frequent cutting is fine for hedging plants and topiary as the more often you trim during a summer season, the more quickly they will grow, pushing out new shoots at the cutting point. This applies particularly to new plantings of box and yew. I call this trimming or cutting, not pruning.

So we prune and cut for many reasons. To give a plant good shape. To keep a plant healthy by removing dead or diseased growth. To allow light and air to reach the centre of a plant and encourage flowering. To relieve the plant of seed formation by dead-heading flowers as soon as they fade. To train plants to grow to take advantage of garden space and light. To provide a framework of fruiting or flowering spurs. We sometimes cut back side shoots on young trees to encourage a sturdy main trunk.

SHAPING BOX to a mushroom dome is best done with sharp, ordinary shears. Wet the box leaves first using a watering-can with a rose attached. For more intricate topiary, it may be necessary to make a wooden frame to guide the cutter.

SHAPING PLANTS

Many shrubs have such beautiful natural shapes that pruning should be kept to a minimum and successful pruning becomes an art. The winter appearance of well-trained roses can be as strikingly beautiful as the summer appearance. Fruit trained in decorative ways, either free-standing or against a wall, will add class to any garden but needs a degree of technical skill. Not all shrubs benefit from being cut and shaped. With the cultivars of elegant shrubs such as *Viburnum plicatum* pruning should be light or else the natural horizontal branching habit will be lost. Give these sort of shrubs and small trees such the Asian dogwood (*Cornus controversa*) an open site with plenty of space for development.

When you cut, you stimulate growth at the point

where the cut is made. This is important. You can ruin the grace of arching shrubs, such as shrub roses, by cutting back where they have grown shoots that are too long. If you do this, the plant will have an ugly, tufted appearance. Instead, cut out old wood right from the base, allowing light and air to reach the centre and new, young growth to replace the old.

Remember when shaping shrubs or correcting uneven growth that it is where you prune most heavily that growth will be most stimulated so the cure to uneven growth is to prune lightly on the overgrown side and heavily on the weaker side. This is quite contrary to a natural urge which makes one want to inhibit and control excessive growth by cutting back.

All plants, but particularly woody ones, are

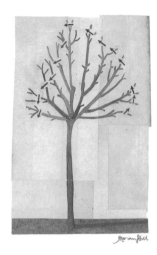

MAINTAINING SYMMETRY for shrubs such as a formal bay tree requires pruning most vigorously where growth is weakest because cutting stimulates growth. If a plant is uneven, prune hard on the weaker side and less on the stronger side and it will soon regain the desired shape.

architectural features in the garden and, up to a point, can be trained and manipulated to create the shapes you want. The basic principles of growing a tree or woody shrub are as follows. A main central leader stem will dominate and often needs the support of a stake when first planted. This leader needs to be well looked after. If it becomes damaged, the structure of the plant is in jeopardy. Removing lower lateral stems in autumn will strengthen the leader. Usually in the first year they will be removed altogether, but in later years only the lowest need to be totally cropped whilst higher laterals need to be cut back. You can give height to plants – lifting their heads – by removing lower stems and branches. This is useful in a small garden allowing a layer of planting around their trunks.

Many shrubs can be trained relatively easily into useful standard shapes with clear stems and round lollipop or globular heads. The French do this better than most. These are not only space-savers, allowing another layer of plants beneath them, but also useful tools in garden design. Currently I am training lemon-scented verbenas as standards in pots, and the Russian olive, *Elaeagnus angustifolia*, to produce globe-shaped heads in my borders, and I am just about to tackle two lemon trees that I grow in pots. A few years ago I visited Helen Dillon's town garden in Dublin and noted how skilled she was at pruning, not only thinning out the centre of shrubs for light and air, but getting their heads up to make the most use of space underneath.

WHEN TO PRUNE

When to prune is as important as why. Avoid pruning when the soil is wet after a rainstorm because standing near the base will compact the soil. Frosty conditions are not good for pruning and the same is true when there are icy winds. Do not prune evergreen shrubs in autumn or in winter as the resultant shoots will be 'zapped' in the first cold spell.

Before pruning any shrub with the aim of improving flowering, find out whether it flowers on old or new wood. Use a good plant manual for this and if necessary go to a library or check with a nursery. Better still, wait to see when it flowers. This knowledge is the most fundamental guide to correct pruning. Old wood is the shoot made in the previous season; new wood is made in the current year. To produce the maximum number of flowers, you need to get to know your plants as individuals.

Most spring-flowering shrubs flower on wood or branches made in the previous year so they should be pruned directly after or while flowering. Prune out all the flowering branches - you can use them for decorating the house - to allow the plants to make plenty of new shoots through the summer months. These new branches will ripen and harden in the sun and produce next spring's buds.

Shrubs that flower later in the summer season can be trimmed and shaped during the winter months, allowing them to send out new shoots to bear flowers the following season. Some shrubs are best pruned when completely dormant, so they will not immediately send out vulnerable new shoots until warmer weather arrives. Others, such as buddleias, forms of *Buddleja davidii* and *B. fallowiana* (but not cascading *B.alternifolia*) and climbers including later summer-flowering clematis, are cut back very hard in late winter before new buds are being formed. In variable climates, when winter and spring warm spells are frequently followed by cold snaps, pruning of many deciduous shrubs is best completed before spring sap rises, even before Christmas if possible.

Flowers and shape are not the only considerations for pruning. We grow some deciduous shrubs for their interesting scarlet, golden or glaucous bark to be admired in winter. Coloured-stemmed dogwoods and willows can be cut almost to the ground or pollarded back to a main trunk in early spring. These new stems are most colourful the following

19

EARLY SUMMER-FLOWERING shrubs such as philadelphus are pruned directly after flowering. Cut flowering
shoots back hard and remove dead wood from the base.

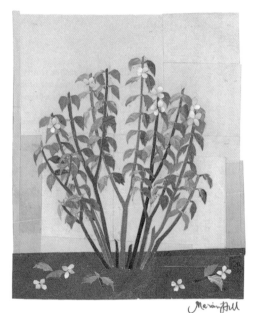

IN THE MONTHS that follow the shrub will make new branches where is has been pruned. It is these branches that will produce flowers the following year.

winter. I usually cut half the old growth of Cornus alba types every other year rather than the whole bush each season but willows look best when pollarded annually to a five or six foot trunk.

Evergreens should be pruned in spring or summer when there is no danger of frost to soft new growth. Evergreen shrubs grown for foliage as well as flora effects, such as Brachyglottis Sunshine, lavender, santolina, germander, woody salvias and most of the silvers, can be pruned at the end of April with the more tender deciduous shrubs such as caryopteris. Even if you prune to a correct timetable, a warm, wet autumn encourages new growth which, unhardened, will be at risk from winter frost and plants that do receive winter damage will need additional tidying, in late spring.

Marian Bull

LATE-SUMMER shrubs such as most buddleias flower on that year's growth. Prune back to two buds in late winter/early spring. Shorten branches any time after flowering.

23

Some *genera* need careful studying as not all of the *genus* have the same pruning needs. With clematis, for example, it would be wise to obtain a pruning manual telling you how to treat each of the three basic types. But even with clematis, common sense will give you more than a hint. Those that flower in spring, such as *Clematis armandii* and all the *alpina*, *macropetala* and *montana* types, are trimmed up after flowering, but only if necessary. Later-flowerers, such as *C. viticella* are cut down to two buds in spring. For large-flowered clematis, take individual advice. But don't be dogmatic. Sometimes you can control flowering times by cutting half a plant at one time and half at another to prolong its performance. One year I forgot to cut down my *Clematis* 'Bill MacKenzie', normally a late-summer flowerer, which

I grow through a spring-flowering ceanothus. It flowered with the ceanothus - a spectacular yellow and blue combination.

The rose is another pruning complexity, requiring understanding of the various kinds of roses, all of which need different pruning priorities. However, the general rules of pruning apply and when followed, even rose bushes are easily manageable as you get to know their individual ways. Although container-grown roses are available and can be planted at any time of year, most roses are offered bare-root for winter planting. All newly-planted roses should be pruned back to two or three buds at planting time or in the following March. In succeeding years different rose types require slightly different techniques.

Like other shrubs, roses fall into two distinct cat-

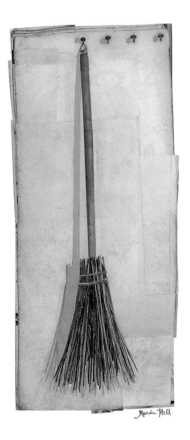

egories: those that flower on the current year's growth and those producing flowers on the previous year's shoots. The former, which includes hybrid tea and bush roses, can be pruned towards the end of winter, anytime from January to March, cutting back more or less hard according to type and with an eye on the shape required. The latter, which includes climbing hybrid teas and climbing floribundas as well as ramblers and climbers in general and shrub roses, should be pruned immediately after flowering or in the winter months, care being taken to preserve the branches and stems of new growth for flowering. Shrub roses should have old wood removed from the base to open out the centre of the bush, leaving arching branches of newer wood to make a graceful shape. Roses that produce beautiful fruits should be left until winter. Tender roses such as *Rosa bracteata* and its hybrid 'Mermaid' always need tidying up after cold winters and *R. banksiae* flowers best if shaped and cut back after flowering is over in the spring.

There are other general guidelines to follow before reaching for the specialist manual for your types of roses and they apply to many shrubs. At any time of the year, cut back diseased wood to a point where the pith of the stem is white. Any dead wood should be removed completely whenever possible. Shoots rising at the base or below main growth, usually with pale leaves and with a different leaf and thorn shape to the main rose, are suckers and must be removed from below ground level immediately they appear.

Dead-heading roses is similarly general in application. As soon as a flower fades, the energy of the rose plant is inhibited by hormones which start the process of forming hips to contain seeds. Removal of dead flowers is essential for healthy rose plants. The best way to do this is with secateurs, cutting the rose head and stem down to the next new shoot and at times cutting off an entire truss of blooms, such as are found in bush roses.

Wisteria requires the same regime no matter what the variety. Once established it needs attention in July and February, cutting back new lateral stems to about 15 cm (6 in) in summer, and then further pruning the same growths to 10 cm (4in) in winter. Although flowering may be the first consideration, when pruning climbers such as wisteria it is also

WISTERIA IS PRUNED twice annually. In July, once the plant is established, the young extension growths need to be trimmed back to approximately 15 cm (6 in) in length, leaving four or six leaves on the young stems. These growths should then be guided on to the frame.

THE SECOND PRUNING is done in winter when the same
shoots that were cut back in the summer are cut again. This
time cut the stems back to approximately 7.5 cm or 10 cm
(3 in or 4 in) and leaving two or three buds for the next
year's growth.

31

MAKING THE CUT

When pruning, it is also important to make a correct cut. The first step is to ensure you have the right equipment and that it is sharp. Secateurs are essential and it is worth investing in those of better quality. A pruning knife, which folds its curved blade into the wooden handle, is not easy to use and can make untidy cuts but is extremely useful for tidying cuts if kept clean and keenly sharp. Long-handled secateurs for climbers and tall plants, called loppers, are very useful though it must be remembered that, as with normal secateurs, they will not cut happily through stems more than 3.5cm (1$\frac{1}{2}$ in) thick, though the stronger double-action loppers will tackle sturdier stems. A pruning saw is also advisable and the most useful are those which are curved with teeth on one

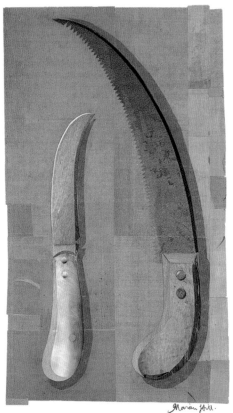

Marian Hill.

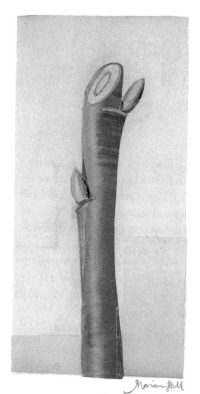

36

side only so that the cut occurs as you withdraw the blade. Cut slowly with a saw and use patience rather than strength to avoid tearing stems. For trimming, it is essential to have sharp shears or a powered hedge-trimmer for extensive hedgerows.

Make a slanting cut above a strong bud and sloping the cut down toward the bud. Do not cut too close to the bud, nor too far from it – ideally the cut should end not more than 0.5 cm ($\frac{1}{4}$ in) above a bud. Make a cut clean, always avoiding stripping bark or tearing a stem. If this occurs, correct the tear as neatly as possible. Using a sharp tool and a decisive action is the best way to prevent untidy cuts. Woods

CUT clean on a slant. Straight cuts may encourage disease.

vary and it is not always the width of a stem that will indicate its resistance to a blade. If a blade will not bite, it is best to withdraw immediately and avoid all temptation to use a twisting action that will damage both blade and plant. Turn to a saw or a strong lopper when secateurs will not suffice.

My husband, John Malins, used to do all the pruning at Tintinhull. In fact, he didn't trust me to get it right nor to do it hard enough. He liked to quote Christopher Lloyd's adage that a bad time to prune is when you do not have time to do it properly. On the whole he taught me to be more drastic. During the first two years in my new garden on my own, I let things rip. Now I think I'm getting things sorted. My walled garden here at Bettiscomb is only 40 x 40 m (110 x 110 ft) and stuffed with shrubs including many broadleaf evergreens which are my chief gardening focus. Most of these are cut and trimmed in late spring. I probably give pruning for shape priority over pruning for the production of flowers. In this small garden it is important to make extra space by raising the heads of many of both the deciduous and the evergreen shrubs. Smoke bushes, elaeagnus and branching philadelphus are ideal host plants to twining clematis and their leafless canopies provide perfect shelter to early spring bulbs.

Evergreen escallonias, choisyas, phillyreas and *Bupleurum fruticosum* provide winter architecture but need some shaping for their all-the-year-round appearance. Forms of woody phlomis can be cut down to the ground in spring if they get too ungainly; this will delay flowering but will improve appearances. I grow six specimens of my favourite ever-green tree, *Phillyrea latifolia*; two I am allowing to mature to natural tree-shapes - it is a small tree even at maturity - keeping their heads raised and allowing them to create drifts of shade beneath in which hellebores and snowdrops thrive. The other four are grown as clipped architectural pyramids, a nice foil to more rounded bushes and the soft flowing lines of perennials and annuals, but creating much less shade and taking up much less space. I trim these phillyreas after they have flowered in April.

RULES AND RECOMMENDATIONS

I don't bother cultivating troublesome climbing roses which need careful thinning out and training – I use my walls for tender evergreens and climbers - but I do grow the more relaxed rambling roses, which I encourage to cover metal arches which frame some of the paths. Pruning at the recommended times is difficult as I grow late-flowering clematis through them (and through all my wall shrubs). The late-small-flowering clematis (mainly *viticella* types) add enormously to my garden's flower-power, especially as most of the ramblers only flower once. A good example is *Clematis* 'Huldine', that twines through a white Banksian rose on my warmest wall. The rose needs hard pruning after spring flowering just at the moment when the 'Huldine' is already thrusting vig-

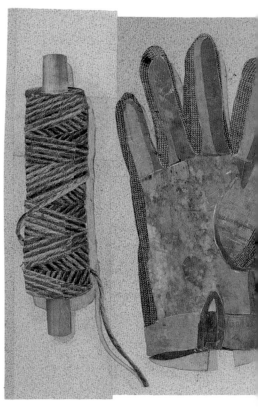

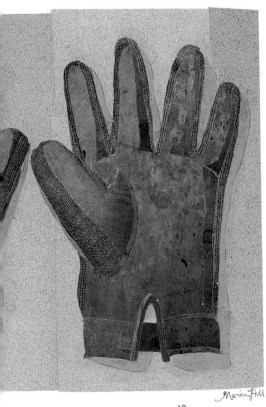

Marian Hill

43

orously upwards.

Remember that the uncut shrub often continues to perform year after year, in spite of prescriptive recommendations in the pruning manuals. Philadelphus is a case in point. I find you need to prune only to keep it healthy and within bounds, but when I do prune it, I feed and cut immediately after flowering in strict textbook fashion.

I find trimming and shaping plants interesting and enjoy the exertion, especially in winter. In summer I often neglect cutting out flowering branches of the early spring-flowerers. Probably the task comes when there are too many other demands on one's time. Of course they would be better if cut regularly but they still flower well and look good to me. So don't let the rules of pruning by the book, get you down; it is not always necessary. Even fussy plants such as clematis and wisteria will continue to be healthy and flower if they miss their prescribed cut and trim. Many gardens maintained by insensitive contractors get a brisk topping in late winter, leaving spring and summer -flowering shrubs such as deutzias, spiraeas and philadelphus as twigs in the soil with no hope of flower production in that season.

The ordinary gardener can anticipate flowering schedules for each plant and follow common sense rules. It is always a comfort to remember that it is better not to prune at all, than to do it in a half-hearted fashion or in the wrong way.

ACKNOWLEDGEMENTS

ILLUSTRATIONS by Marian Hill
DESIGNED by Roger Walton
PRODUCTION by Imago Publishing Ltd

Photograph of Penelope Hobhouse by Charles Hopkinson

First published in Great Britain by John Brown Publishing Ltd,
The New Boathouse, 136-142 Bramley Road, London
W10 6SR

ISBN 1-902212-282

Printed and bound in China for Imago

GARDENS

ILLUSTRATED

Take out a SPECIAL OFFER subscription to the world's leading gardening magazine. Only £29.50 for 10 issues, a saving of 15%.

I would like to take out a subscription to GARDENS ILLUSTRATED

☐ 1 year (10 issues): £29.50 UK; £45.00 Europe, £60.00 rest of world

☐ 2 years (20 issues): £58.00 UK; £89.00 Europe, £110.00 rest of world

☐ I enclose a cheque payable to John Brown Publishing (sterling cheques only)

for £ _____

I would like to pay by credit/debit card. Please charge my:

☐ VISA ☐ MASTERCARD ☐ AMEX ☐ EUROCARD

☐ CONNECT ☐ SWITCH: issue no./start date [_____]

Card Number ☐☐☐☐ ☐☐☐☐ ☐☐☐☐ ☐☐☐☐

Expiry Date ☐☐☐☐

Signature _____ Date _____

Name _____

Address _____

_____ Postcode _____

Telephone _____ Email _____

Send this form to: GARDENS ILLUSTRATED, SUBSCRIPTIONS, FREEPOST (SWB837), BRISTOL BS32 0ZZ (No stamp needed in the UK). Or phone 01454 618 905.

Money back guarantee: you may cancel your subscription at any time if not completely satisfied and receive a refund on all unmailed issues.

GARDENS ILLUSTRATED is published by John Brown Publishing Ltd, The New Boathouse,136-142 Bramley Road, London W10 6SR

CUT ALONG HERE